Get into Science

YOU AND YOUR BODY

Jane Lacey and Sernur Isik

W

Franklin Watts
First published in Great Britain in 2020 by The Watts Publishing Group

Credits
Design and project management: Raspberry Books
Art Direction: Sidonie Beresford-Browne
Designer: Kathryn Davies
Consultant: Sally Nankivell-Aston
Illustrations: Sernur Isik

HB ISBN: 978 1 4451 7018 3
PB ISBN: 978 1 4451 7019 0

Printed in Dubai

FSC
www.fsc.org

MIX
Paper from
responsible sources
FSC® C104740

Franklin Watts
An imprint of
Hachette Children's Group
Part of The Watts Publishing Group
Carmelite House
50 Victoria Embankment
London EC4Y 0DZ

An Hachette UK Company
www.hachette.co.uk

www.franklinwatts.co.uk

CONTENTS

Have a look at yourself in the mirror. Every part of your body that you can see has a name.

head

hand

finger

arm

elbow

chest

We have named some of the parts of the body on this page. **What other parts can you name?**

knee

leg

foot

4

Different parts of your body often work together.

✋ TRY IT OUT!

Bend down and take off your shoe. You used your eyes to see your shoe and your hands to take it off. **Which other parts of your body did you move and use?**

Each part of your body is in the right place and is a good shape for the special job it does.

You use your hands for holding a paint brush.

How else do you use your hands and feet?

You walk, run and jump on your feet.

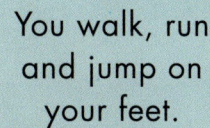

💡 THINK ABOUT IT!

Your eyes are in a good place for seeing. Imagine what it would be like if your eyes were in the back of your head!

YOU ARE SPECIAL!

Martha, Toby, Ellie and Jack look different from each other. They all enjoy doing different things.

You are special, too. No one else in the world is exactly the same as you. What do you enjoy doing? What are you good at?

Everyone is different, but we all have lots of things that are the same. What things are the same about you, Martha, Toby, Ellie and Jack? How do your bodies work?

Usually you can recognise someone straight away just by looking at them. People are different sizes.

Hair, skin and eyes can all be different colours.

What else can be different about the way people look?

THINK ABOUT IT!

No one else in the world has the same thoughts as you or knows what you are thinking.

Voices are different, too. You might recognise someone's voice on the telephone.

 TRY IT OUT!

Collect some facts about your friends like this.
Do any friends have the same answers to all four questions? How similar are they in other ways?

	Colour of hair	Colour of eyes	Size of feet	Favourite food
			12	ice cream
Ellie	brown	brown		

MAKING SENSE!

How do you think Maddy knows that the apple is delicious, the teddy bear feels soft and that her t-shirt is yellow? She uses her senses.

Senses let you see, hear, smell, taste and feel what is going on around you.

You see with your eyes, hear with your ears, smell with your nose, taste with your tongue and feel with your skin.

Your brain is inside your head.
It makes sense of the world around you.

Nerves connect your brain to the rest of your body. They take messages to your brain all the time about what you can see, hear, smell, taste and feel.

If you pick up something too hot, like this drink, you put it down quickly.

Sometimes important messages are sent to your brain to keep you safe.

A warning message is sent from your fingers to your brain that the mug – and the drink – might burn you!

OUCH!

SAFETY WARNING!

Always take extra care when picking up hot drinks.

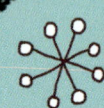

EATING
and
DRINKING

A delicious smell from a plate of food makes you feel hungry! You need food to give you energy, to keep warm, to grow and to stay healthy.

carbohydrates

protein

Food can be put into four groups:

fruit and vegetables

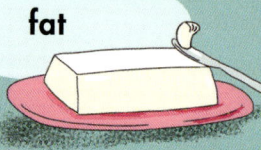

fat

You should eat some food from all of these groups to get the goodness you need each day. You need to drink plenty of water, too.

10

THINK ABOUT IT!

Do you have food from each of these groups every day? Do you eat more food from one group than another?

Think about what happens to your food next time you have something to eat.

First you chew it up into smaller bits – then you swallow it.

The mashed-up food goes down into your stomach. Here, juices in your stomach make the food even smaller so that your body can take the good parts from it.

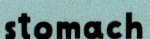
stomach

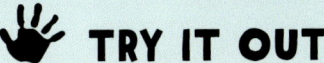 TRY IT OUT!

Chew a mouthful of food. Can you feel slippery saliva in your mouth helping it to slip down? Feel your neck when you swallow – your food has started on its journey through your body.

When you go to the toilet, your body gets rid of the parts of the food it cannot use.

KEEPING HEALTHY

Usually, you feel fit and well. There are plenty of things you can do to stay that way. Germs can make you feel ill. They are too small to see, so you have to be careful not to catch them!

Germs stick to your hands, so always wash them before you eat. Germs in your stomach can make you feel sick.

Cold germs make you cough and sneeze. Use a handkerchief so no one else catches your germs!

 **LOOK AGAIN!**

Look again at page 10 to find something else you can do to help you to keep healthy.

Often, when you feel ill, rest will soon make you better. Sometimes you need medicine to help your body to fight germs. You may go to the doctor or nurse for this medicine.

A doctor, or nurse may give you an injection, too. An injection protects you from a disease, so it helps you stay healthy.

If you have an accident you might have to go to hospital. Hospitals give you special treatment, like an operation or mending a broken arm.

THINK ABOUT IT!

Have you ever been ill or had an accident? How did you feel? What did you do to get better?

13

SKIN

Skin makes a very good covering for your body. It stretches when you move, it keeps out germs, it is waterproof, and helps to keep you warm in the cold and cool in the heat.

Melanin is a dark colour in your skin that helps to protect you from sun-burn. The darker your skin, the more melanin you have.

! SAFETY WARNING

Don't forget to wear a hat and use sun-tan cream to protect you when you play in the sun.

Your skin is sensitive – you touch and feel things with it. The skin on your fingertips is very sensitive.

Washing helps to keep germs away and keeps your skin clean and healthy.

What else do you do to keep your body clean?

Blind or visually impaired people read with their fingertips. They use them to feel letters made up of little bumps.

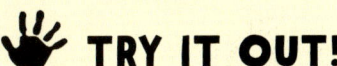 **TRY IT OUT!**

Pick up different things and feel them. Do they feel rough or smooth? Are they warm or cold to touch? What else does your sense of touch tell you about them?

UNDER the SKIN

skull →

Your **shoulders** are joints too. Move your arm. Can you make it go round and round? What other joints can you find?

ribs

Can you feel the strong, hard bones under your skin? Bones give your body its shape.

You have **206 bones** joined together by joints. Joints let you bend and move.

spine (back bone)

TRY IT OUT!

Your knees are joints. Bend them. Can you feel how they move backwards and forwards like hinges on a door?

Your bones and skin protect the parts of your body you cannot see. These are the parts of you that make your body work day and night.

These are just some of the parts inside your body. Each one has a special job to do.

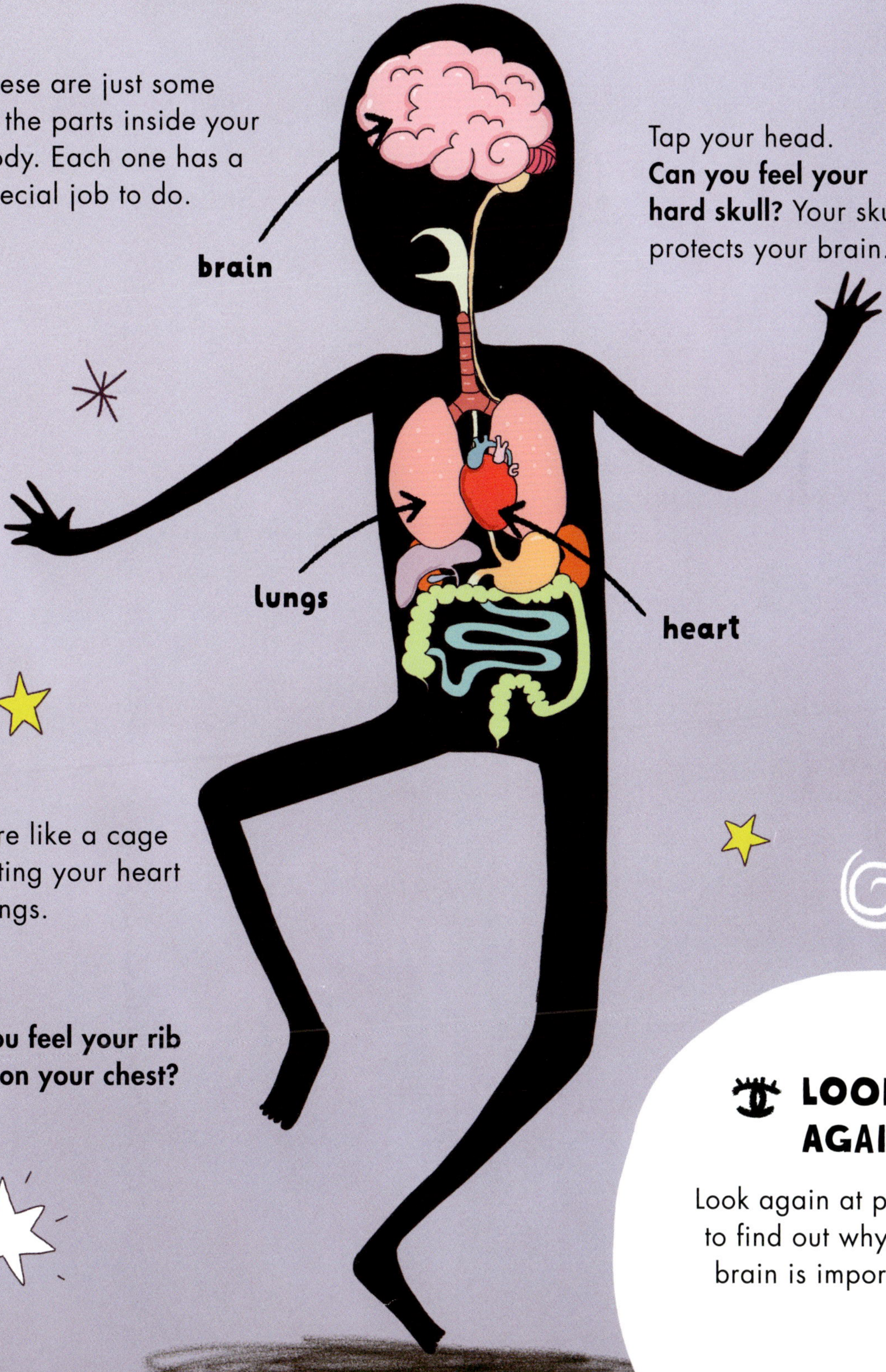

brain

Tap your head. **Can you feel your hard skull?** Your skull protects your brain.

lungs

heart

Ribs are like a cage protecting your heart and lungs.

Can you feel your rib bones on your chest?

LOOK AGAIN

Look again at page 9 to find out why your brain is important.

17

BREATHING

Look at all the different things the people in these pictures are doing. They are all breathing air in and out of their lungs, even the boy who is asleep.

Your body needs oxygen from the air all the time – that's why you can't hold your breath for very long.

THINK ABOUT IT!

Why is it difficult to stay under water for very long when you go swimming?

You breathe fresh air in through your nose and mouth. Breathe in and feel your chest getting bigger as your lungs fill with air.

You breathe stale air out through your nose and mouth, too. Breathe out.

Can you feel your body pushing out the stale air?

✋ TRY IT OUT!

Dangle a tissue in front of your face.
Breathe deeply and watch the tissue move away from you as you breathe out, and then towards you as you breathe in.

PUMPING
BLOOD

Look at the inside of your wrists. Can you see some blue coloured tubes under the skin? These are blood vessels. They carry blood all around your body.

Your blood does a very important job. It collects oxygen from your lungs and takes it to every part of your body. It also carries all the goodness and energy from the food you eat around your body.

Have you ever cut yourself and seen your own red blood? Blood helps your cut to heal.

You should wash your cut to help keep out the germs.

Your blood will dry into a scab that covers the cut, while your skin mends underneath.

Put your hand on your chest. Can you feel your heart beat? Your heart is doing its job. It pumps your blood to every part of your body.

When you are exercising you need more energy from your blood, so your heart works harder.

Your heart never stops working, day and night, so your blood never stops moving all around your body.

 TRY IT OUT!

Feel your heart beat when you are sitting or standing still. Now run, jump or skip for a minute or two. Feel your heart again. What do you notice?

21

ON the MOVE

Did you know that every time you move you use your muscles? You use muscles to move your arms and legs. You use muscles to bite and chew. You even use muscles when you smile or blink.

Muscles are attached to your bones by strong cords called tendons. You can feel a big tendon, called the Achilles tendon, in the back of your leg, just above your heel.

You have big, strong muscles attached to the bones in your legs. These muscles pull the bones in your leg when you bend, walk or run.

 TRY IT OUT!

Bend your knees up and down.
Feel what happens to the muscles above your knees and in the back of your legs as you move.

Exercise makes your muscles work hard and keeps them strong and healthy.

 **LOOK AGAIN**

Look again at page 21.
What happens to your heart when you exercise?

SLEEP WELL

Your heart never stops beating, you never stop breathing and your brain never stops working. But sometimes your body needs to rest.

You need plenty of sleep to stay healthy.

As you sleep through the night, your body doesn't have to work so hard. You breathe more slowly and your heart beats less quickly.

The brain is quite active at working out problems while you sleep which is why you sometimes have an 'ah' moment when you wake up.

Your muscles get a rest from moving about.

Sleep gives your body time to get better when you are ill.

After a good night's sleep, you wake up ready for another busy day. Sleep is a good time for growing, too.

How many hours' sleep do you usually have at night? Ask an adult how many hours they usually sleep. **Who has the most sleep?**

THINK ABOUT IT!

Why do babies need so much sleep?

25

USEFUL
WORDS

BLOOD

Blood is the red liquid that carries oxygen from your lungs and goodness from your food to every part of your body.

BLOOD VESSELS

Your blood travels all round your body through tubes called blood vessels.

BONES

Bones are strong and hard. They make a frame to support your body called a skeleton.

BRAIN

You think with your brain and make sense of the world around you with your brain.

DISEASE

A disease makes you feel ill. Sometimes an injection can protect you from catching a disease.

ENERGY

People use energy from food to keep warm, grow and move.

GERMS

Germs carry diseases which can make you feel ill. Germs are too tiny to see.

HEART

Your heart is a strong muscle that pumps blood all around your body. It works all the time.

JOINTS

Joints are the places where your bones are joined together. They let your body bend and move. Knees and elbows are joints.

LUNGS

You have two lungs that are like bags inside your chest. They fill up with air when you breathe in, and empty when you breathe out.

MELANIN

Melanin is a dark colour in your skin that helps to protect you from sun-burn. The darker your skin, the more melanin you have.

MUSCLES

Muscles are attached to your bones so you can move them. Other muscles help you breathe and swallow food. Your heart is a muscle that pumps blood.

NERVES

Nerves connect your brain to the rest of your body. They take messages to and from your brain about what you sense and do.

OXYGEN

Oxygen is a kind of gas that is part of the air we breathe. Our bodies need oxygen to work.

RIBS

Your ribs are the bones that make a cage that protects your heart and lungs.

SALIVA

Saliva is a liquid that is made in your mouth. It starts to break down the food in your mouth and helps it to slip down when you swallow it.

SENSES

Seeing, hearing, feeling, smelling and tasting are the five senses. You use your senses to tell what is going on all around you.

SKULL

Your skull is the bone in your head that protects your brain and gives your head its shape.

STOMACH

When you eat, your food goes into your stomach where juices break it down into very tiny pieces.

TENDONS

Tendons are strong cords that attach your muscles to your bones.

QUIZ

Now it's time to see how much you have learned. Try out this quick quiz to test your knowledge.

1 **What is the name of the part of your body you use to see?**

a) Hand
b) Eyes
c) Knee

2 **How many senses do we have?**

a) Five
b) Two
c) Nine

3 **Which of our body parts do we use to taste?**

a) Ears
b) Eyes
c) Tongue

4 **The four groups food are fat, carbohydrates, protein and what?**

a) Drinks
b) Sugar and spice
c) Fruit and vegetables

5 **Where does our food go once we have swallowed it?**

a) Into our stomach
b) Into our hands
c) Into our lungs

6 What is one of the ways we can avoid spreading germs?

a) Blowing on our hands
b) Washing our hands before we eat
c) Clapping our hands

7 Which of these body parts is made up of bones?

a) Skull
b) Brain
c) Lungs

8 Which of these pumps blood to every part of our body?

a) Ribs
b) Liver
c) Heart

9 What is the name of the strong cords which attach your muscles to your bones?

a) Tentacles
b) Tendons
c) Tissues

10 What can we do that will help our bodies rest, heal and grow?

a) Dance
b) Run
c) Sleep

FURTHER INFORMATION

BOOKS TO READ

- *BOOM! Science: Human Body* by Georgie Amson-Bradshaw (Wayland 2018)
- *Science in Action: Your Body and Science in Action: Your Bones* by Sally Hewitt (QED 2018)
- *My Amazing Body Machine* by Robert Winston (DK Children 2017)

WEBSITES TO VISIT

- **Go to BBC Bitesize: Human Body** to find out more about all the topics in this book. www.bbc.co.uk/bitesize/topics/z9yycdm
- Take a journey through the digestive system with **National Geographic Kids**: www.natgeokids.com/uk/discover/science/general-science/your-digestive-system/

ATTRACTIONS TO EXPLORE

Visit **Eureka! The National Children's Museum** in Halifax to explore interactive exhibits all about you and your body. Head to **W5** in Belfast to discover all about the human body through their hands-on exhibition, then test your strength in their multi-storey climbing structure **Climbit!** Pop into London's **Science Museum** to find out how your body works, investigate how genetics play a part and discover lots more.

NOTE TO PARENTS AND TEACHERS

ABOUT THIS BOOK

Children are natural scientists. They learn by touching and feeling, noticing, asking questions and trying things out for themselves. The books in the *Get into Science!* series are designed for the way children learn. Familiar objects are used as starting points for further learning. *You and Your Body* starts with thinking about food and explores how the body works.

Each double page spread introduces a new topic, such as skin. Information is given, questions asked and activities suggested that encourage children to make discoveries and develop new ideas for themselves. Look out for these panels throughout the book:

TRY IT OUT! indicates a simple activity, using safe materials, that proves or explores a point.

THINK ABOUT IT! indicates a question inspired by the information on the page but which points the reader to areas not covered by the book.

LOOK AGAIN introduces a cross-referencing activity which links themes and facts throughout the book.

Encourage children not to take the familiar world for granted. Point things out, ask questions and enjoy making scientific discoveries together.

INDEX